THE
FLAME
OF
LOVE

THE
FLAME
OF
LOVE

RUMI'S 100 MOST
PASSIONATE POEMS

MUHAMMAD ALI MOJARADI

MANDALA

San Rafael Los Angeles London

For my parents, Farīd and Mahnāz, who encouraged me to pursue my passions, however outlandish they were, instead of turning me into a doctor, lawyer, or engineer by force.

For my late grandmother, Ashraf al-Sādāt Banī-Jamālī, who taught me to read Persian, and my grandfather, Muhammad Mujarradī, who, with his no-nonsense, working-class attitude, taught me eloquence (*adab*) in accordance with Saʿdi's dictum, "I learned *adab* from those with no *adab*!"

For my *yār* and *nūr-i chashm*, Sayyida Shīrīn.

CONTENTS

ON TRANSLITERATION

The question of transliterating Persian and Arabic words is complex and occasionally controversial. Most readers will only encounter Persian transliteration in the case of proper nouns, often written by laypersons. You may meet your friend Mohammad from Qom for some kebab koobideh, or is that Muhammad, Qum, and kabab kubide? Do Iranian Jews celebrate Hanukkah in Esfahan or Chanukah in Isfahan?

Native speakers often Latinize Persian in a way that seems intuitive to them, or in a way that sacrifices form for clarity. For example, Rumi's name is often pronounced *rum-ee* by the unfamiliar. Perhaps a more foolproof spelling would be Roomy. Similarly, many a Kāmrān and Shirvīn have spelled their names as Cameron and Sherwin.

Academics transliterate Persian with standardization and backward compatibility in mind. Each Persian letter is assigned a Latin counterpart. This system is followed strictly—whether or not the results are easy to interpret for the uninitiated—which is why we have Rumi instead of Roomie or Roomy.

I have opted for a slightly modified version of the International Journal of Middle East Studies (IJMES) system. Therefore, you may not be accustomed to the spelling of some Persian words. For example, Husayn instead of Hossein or Hussain and Shams al-Din instead of Shamsoddin or Shamsaddin. When words are well established in English, I have opted for the common spelling, such as Mecca and kohl, which should be Makkah and kuhl according to the IJMES system.

Although you can recite Rumi's Persian poetry in any accent, the rhyme scheme occasionally requires you to mimic his native Tajik dialect (also known as Dari). For example, Rumi rhymes the words *khwash* (nice) with *kash* (pull). If you were to read these in a modern Iranian accent (*khush* and *kesh*, respectively), the rhyme would be lost. For this reason, I have based my transliteration on Rumi's native dialect. Speakers of Iranian Persian will notice that *v* is written as *w*, as well as the presence of *majhūl* (unclear) vowels, especially the *yā* and *o* sounds, such that *mī-gūyam* becomes *me-goyam*.

ON RUMI'S LIFE

Muhammad son of Muhammad son of al-Husayn of Balkh, known as Rumi, was born on the cusp of a turbulent era. It was September 1207 CE, just a few years before the Mongols would overrun his hometown and the rest of Central and Western Asia. The young Rumi migrated westward with his immediate family, which spared them the grisly fate of those left behind.

Though he escaped with his life, Rumi was left scarred, yearning for a home that was no longer there. His family eventually settled in Anatolia, in the city of Konya. Rumi's father worked as a midlevel cleric, preaching and teaching in Konya's mosques, preparing Rumi to replace him. But everything changed one fateful day when Rumi met Shams al-Din-i Tabrizi, known as Shams.

Shams was born in northwestern Iran a few decades before Rumi. He showed spiritual prowess early on—once relating that he would fast for days as a small child, leaving his parents puzzled. After completing seminary studies and spiritual instruction, Shams set off to find the greatest mystics of his day, but none of them quenched his thirst.

Eventually, Shams arrived in Damascus, where a young Rumi had traveled to pursue his own seminary studies. When Shams saw Rumi, he approached him and exclaimed, "Oh, money changer of the world, find me!"[1] before disappearing back into the crowd.

Though Rumi was still raw, Shams recognized that Rumi would become the great mystic he'd been seeking once he was cooked by the flame of love—a flame that Shams would kindle. Shams disappeared for over a decade before returning to find an older Rumi in Konya.

From the moment Rumi and Shams were reunited, the two of them were inseparable, often secluded together for days at a time. Rumi and Shams were previously unremarkable and likely would have been relegated to obscure footnotes in historical texts, were they remembered at all. But their powerful union changed their fates, birthing a love story that echoed through the ages, immortalizing them in hearts and minds the world over.

No one knows exactly what unfolded between Rumi and Shams. Historical anecdotes are more hagiography than biography, and modern retellings are more fan fiction than history. What we can glean from Rumi's writing is that

---

1. In the medieval world, money changers were experts at discerning real gold and silver coins (metaphorically, the truth) from counterfeit ones (falsehood).

Shams's teachings were totally transformative. Rumi was already advanced in the exterior sciences (what we'd call Islamic studies today), but Shams taught that academic learning could only lead one to the gates of the spiritual realm. Once arrived, the seeker must cast aside books and traditional learning in order to gain entrance. In that spiritual realm, which even Rumi struggles to describe, knowledge is of an entirely different kind.

Rumi's disciples and family members may have been envious of this relationship and suspicious of Shams's unorthodox approach to religion. Some write that they threatened Shams, causing his disappearance. As the months turned to years, Rumi despaired, but eventually word arrived that Shams had been spotted in Damascus. Rumi brought Shams back, turning his heartbreak into joy.

Both men fell to their knees at their emotional reunion. No one could tell lover and beloved apart.[2] The forlorn Rumi then concocted a plan to keep Shams in Konya for good. Shams would marry Rumi's new stepdaughter, Kimiya, and join the household. The marriage ended with Kimiya's natural death. Not long after that, Shams disappeared for a final time.

2. In Sufism, the student is a lover and the teacher is the beloved.

Legend says that Shams was killed by Rumi's estranged son ʿAla al-Din, who may have secretly loved Kimiya. Others say Shams had nothing left to teach Rumi but the pain of separation. Rumi was engrossed in Shams's persona, perhaps so much that he couldn't look past his teacher and find God. Shams may have left so Rumi would reach enlightenment in his absence. Whatever the reason, Shams was gone.

This disappearance turned Rumi into an ecstatic mystic. He began to yearn for a return, like many refugees or émigrés, but he also realized what most of us don't: Our home isn't here; our return is an ascent. His spiritual enlightenment attracted a group of mostly working-class disciples, including women, Christians, and other marginalized people. Rumi's critics thought it improper for a scholar to associate with what they saw as rabble. Free from pretense or care for worldly status, Rumi didn't mind having smiths, farmers, and other simple folk around him.

For those of us who live in liberalized societies where religion, race, and social class largely aren't seen as barriers to friendship and learning, it may be difficult for us to appreciate the depth of Rumi's openness. But consider a world where women and religious minorities were second-class, where peasants and low-skill workers couldn't even look at a noble's face. It was in such a world that Rumi said gender, nobility, and even religion weren't a barrier to his companionship and mystical teaching.

Rumi harshly criticized men who tyrannized women, likening them to animals. Conversely, in one passage, he compares women to God because of their ability to create life. Rumi also rejected religious supremacy, emphasizing the divine source of all religions. In one famous episode, Rumi chastised his Muslim followers for insulting the faith of a Greek Christian.

At that time, spirituality was an elitist affair. Many Sufis thought of themselves as the select few lucky enough to understand divine secrets. Their writings were purposefully arcane. Rumi rejected this elitism, opting to democratize Sufism and explain the deepest spiritual realities in everyday language. He would often draw metaphors from simple, mundane things—like a mill stone or manure—so much so that many have mistaken his deepest passages for children's stories or crude humor.

Rumi's poetry was not conventional in any sense of the word. He would spontaneously recite poems—sometimes while whirling—with disciples in tow recording his utterances. Rumi wasn't a poet before meeting Shams, and he never became one in the professional sense, even after writing thousands of compositions. He often did away with basic conventions such as rhyme and meter, repeating himself ad nauseam, as an ecstatic would. Eventually, his love poems began to number in the thousands. At the insistence of Husam al-Din Chalabi, Rumi then wrote his magnum opus, the *Masnawī-i Maʿnawī* (*Spiritual Couplets*), a long narrative that kept him occupied until death.

Rumi left the world on December 17, 1273 CE. His followers organized themselves into a Sufi community called the Mawlawiyya (Mevlevi in Turkish), which exists to this day. These disciples celebrate his death, which they call *Shab-iʿUrs,* or *The Wedding Night.* To them, Rumi's death isn't a sad event, but a reunion with the beloved. Every December, Rumi's mausoleum becomes a place of music and dance, rather than eulogy and mourning.

Volumes could be written about Rumi's life and his relationship with Shams, but I will leave you with this brief introduction and let the poetry speak for itself. As Rumi said, "I limit myself to this little, for a little is a taste of the much, a mouthful is a sample of the spring water, and a handful is a sample of the harvest."

ON THE POEMS IN THIS BOOK

After Shams's disappearance, Rumi wrote a collection of lyric poetry entitled *Dīwān-i Shams* (*Poetry by Shams*). He believed the work wasn't his, but that of his guide speaking through him.

The *Diwan* contains poems written in several modes, most commonly the *ghazal*—of which there are about 3,200. The ghazal's structure is similar to that of a sonnet, and it is primarily a love lyric, as indicated by its approximate English meaning, *to flirt*.

The second most common mode in the *Diwan* is the *rubāʿī*, a four-line poem similar to an English quatrain— of which there are about 2,000. Sadly, despite Rumi's popularity, the rubāʿī poems of the *Diwan* have received relatively little attention in either the original Persian or in English translation. When I discovered this discrepancy, I decided to translate them myself. After reading them several times over, I rose-picked the contents of this volume, as we say in Persian. May you enjoy it.

—Muhammad Ali Mojaradi

Istanbul

YEARNING
FOR LOVE

ALL OF THE PAGES FROM THE EAST AND WEST,*
I filled with these laments from my pained breast.
A moment spent in love is worth the world.
For love may many souls be laid to rest.

* NOTE: Literally, Cairo (west) and Baghdad (east), both centers of
Islamic learning, hosting al-Azhar University and the Nizāmiyya
Madrasa, respectively.

FIRST LINE IN PERSIAN: *man kāghaz-hā-yi miṣr o baghdād ay jān*

OH IDOL, WHEN I SAW YOUR FACE, AT ONCE
love put me in a daze. I lost my way
because of love for you. One day, you'll see.
About me, "Rest in peace!"* is all they'll say.

* NOTE: Literally, "Verily we are from Him and to Him we return."
A Qur'anic phrase about death.

FIRST LINE IN PERSIAN: *tā rū-yi tu rā bidīdam ay but nāgāh*

I CANNOT SEE YOU AS YOU ARE.

Ah! Damn my superficial sight!

My eyes do not deserve your face.

But eyes can't quit the heart's delight.

NOTE: Rumi reminds us to look deeper at the core of matters, not the surface level. There are two layers to each sense—the sensual and spiritual. We have ears that listen to idle talk and ears that can hear spiritual truths, eyes that see distractions and eyes that can witness the beloved. Sufis dim the worldly senses and strengthen the spiritual. Rumi's eyes are still worldly, looking for fleeting things. They are not yet ready to truly perceive Shams in all his beauty.

FIRST LINE IN PERSIAN: *dūr ast naẓar zi tu bahāna īn ast*

THE TALLEST TREES FALL SHORT OF YOUR
   GRAND HEIGHT.
The rose saw you and ripped itself in two.
Take up a mirror for the sake of God.
Have you seen anyone who looks like you?

FORBID THERE BE A BETTER LOVE THAN YOU!

Or any vision better than your face.

In this world and the next, you will suffice.

Wherever beauty's found, it's from your grace.

FIRST LINE IN PERSIAN: *ḥāshā ki ba ʿālam az tu khwash-tar yārīst*

NONE KNOWS A THING ABOUT YOUR KINGLY
  GRACE
until you make them lose their heart and brain.
Whoever sees your face then leaves your side
is mad if this does not drive them insane!

FIRST LINE IN PERSIAN: *kas wāqif-i ān ḥażrat-i shāhāna nashud*

THE WORLD IS LOOKING TO YOUR FACE.
In love, we tear our cloaks in two.*
The wise know, to be sane is not
more sweet than to be crazed by you!

* NOTE: In Rumi's day, Sufis wore cloaks similar to the habit of a
Christian monk. In moments of spiritual ecstasy, they would tear
these cloaks in two from the collar.

FIRST LINE IN PERSIAN: *ay jumla jahān ba rū-yi khūbat nigarān*

IF IN THEIR CHEST A HEART REMAINS,
they cannot live if you're not there.
Insane's the one who would stay sane
when he sees locks of curly hair.

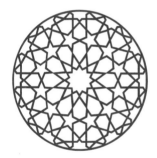

NOTE: In Rumi's day, the clinically insane were committed to asylums, where chains restrained them. In Sufi poetry, love is an ailment that drives the lover mad. Similarly, the beloved's curly ringlets are likened to chains for the crazed lover. When the Arab poet Qays was driven to insanity by Layla, he was given the name Majnūn (literally, "driven mad" or "possessed").

FIRST LINE IN PERSIAN: *dar sīna-yi har ki zarra'ī dil bāshad*

NO LONGER CAN I BEAR MY HEART.
In love, I'll give it all to you.
If I don't give my heart away,
why keep my heart? What does it do?

FIRST LINE IN PERSIAN: *khwad mumkin-i ān nīst ki bar-dāram dil*

WE LOVERS GAMBLE THIS WORLD AND THE
  NEXT.
We gamble centuries—that's just the start.
A thousand days we'll roam in hope of love,
and gamble lives by thousands for one heart.

FIRST LINE IN PERSIAN: *'ushshāq ba yak dam du jahān dar-bāzand*

NOW THAT I'VE BEEN ACQUAINTED WITH
  YOUR LOVE,
so many games of chance play for you.
Oh, won't you prance while tipsy in my heart?
I cleared it out to make a way for you.

FIRST LINE IN PERSIAN: *zān dam ki tu rā ba ʿishq bishnākhtaʾam*

I LEARN TO BE IN LOVE FROM YOUR
   PERFECTION.
Your beauty teaches me to rhyme and write.
Your image dances in my heart all day.
I've learned my whirling from your thought
   and sight.

NOTE: Rumi became a poet after he met Shams.

FIRST LINE IN PERSIAN: *man ʿāshiqī az kamāl-i tu āmozam*

SINCE YOUR LOVE SET MY HEART AFIRE,
all that I had save love was burned.
I set my books and mind aside,
and since then poetry I've learned.

NOTE: Shams encouraged Rumi to abandon traditional learning and embark on a spiritual path of experiential instruction.

FIRST LINE IN PERSIAN: *tā dar dil-i man ʿishq-i tu afrokhta shud*

HIS LOVE CAN STEAL A DOCTOR'S HEART.

What good then can my doctor do?

If he reveals his beauty, then

my doctor will need doctors too!

NOTE: Rumi writes of love as an ailment that requires a skilled physician. The love of Shams is a sickness no doctor can cure.

FIRST LINE IN PERSIAN: *ān yār ki az ṭabīb dil birbāyad*

I SAID, "OH LOVE, WHERE IS YOUR HOME?"

He said, "Inside your ruined heart.

A treasure am I, found in ruins.

So may your home now fall apart!"

NOTE: Treasures are found in ruins. Your home must be destroyed
if you wish to discover spiritual gems there.

FIRST LINE IN PERSIAN: *guftam ki kujā buwad butā khāna-yi tu*

YOU WILL NOT GLANCE MY WAY AT ALL.
You think it's sin, from sin you're free.
My heart wails for your rosy cheeks,
but you won't even sigh for me.

A NORMAL LOVER'S OF NO USE TO ME.
He has no loyalty. He'll only flirt.
A lover is the one who opens wide
the gates of heaven when I'm in the dirt.

NOTE: Rumi doesn't want an ordinary lover and a mundane love
story. He wants a partner who will guide him outside of this
worldly realm.

FIRST LINE IN PERSIAN: *maʿshūqa-yi khānagī ba kārī nāyad*

IF ONE SHOULD CATCH A GLANCE OF YOU
  MY LOVE,

how could another beauty draw his sight?
For someone who has seen you only once,
the sun and moon both seem devoid of light!

FIRST LINE IN PERSIAN: *ān kas ki tu rā dīda buwad ay dil-bar*

BEWILDERED HEART, THERE'S TWO WAYS TO
  THE FRIEND:
one hidden, one apparent. Now, depart.
There is a path on foot, but if it's closed,
another way is found inside your heart.

NOTE: There are two ways to be one with the beloved: the union
of bodies and the union of hearts. Though Shams disappeared, and
was therefore gone in a physical sense, he never left Rumi's heart.
They were always together in a deeper, more meaningful way.

FIRST LINE IN PERSIAN: *sar-gashta dilā ba dost az jān rāhīst*

WHEN THAT FAMED BEAUTY SAW MY SALLOW
   FACE,

he said, "You're not for me. Don't be misled.

For we appear as opposites, it seems.

You're autumn yellow, and I'm springtime red!"

NOTE: Shams discovered Rumi in a state of spiritual depression, while Shams was in spiritual ecstasy. In order to achieve union, Rumi's spiritual state would have to be alive like Shams's. To be red faced is a sign of joy and health. Hence the idiom, "He keeps his face red by slapping it," meaning, "He feigns being in a good state at any cost."

FIRST LINE IN PERSIAN: *chūn dīd rukh-i zard-i man ān shuhra-nigār*

I TOLD MY HEART, "DON'T FALL IN LOVE AGAIN.
Why would you want to open sorrow's door?"
My saddened heart then said, "Oh, righteous man,
look at his beauty. Go, be proud no more!"*

* NOTE: The lover should not be conceited and deny the beloved.

FIRST LINE IN PERSIAN: *bā dil guftam ʿishq-i naw āghāz makun*

I MET A BEAUTY IN THE TAVERN LANE
and bought his love with both my heart and soul.
Once I had smelled the fragrance of his hair,
I lost desire for both the worlds* in whole.

---

* NOTE: This world and the afterlife.

FIRST LINE IN PERSIAN: *dar kū-yi kharābāt nigārī dīdam*

LOVE CAME AND BROKE REPENTANCE* AS IF
  GLASS.
And who can mend a broken glass, oh friends?
Since love can mend all things, not only glass,
how can we flee from love that breaks and mends?

* NOTE: Repentance is *tawba* in Persian. Those with a dry
(*khushk*) understanding of religion swear a vow to renounce
love. When love arrives, that mistaken repentance is broken by
its overwhelming force. Then love will teach us to make a truer,
deeper, more meaningful repentance from this world, which is
the first step on the spiritual path.

FIRST LINE IN PERSIAN: *'ishq āmad o tawba rā chū shīsha bishikast*

FROM WHEN I FIRST LAID EYES UPON YOUR
  FACE,
from your affliction, night and day I cry.
May it be poison if I drink alone.
If I must live without you, may I die!

FIRST LINE IN PERSIAN: *zān roz ki chashm-i man ba rūyat nigarīst*

THE WORK OF LOVERS IS TO SING
about that beauty with no trace.
It's telling tales of snare and bait,
or quitting home and marketplace.

NOTE: Shams often disappeared without a trace. No one would know where he came from or where he was going. The lover is trapped in the snare of love, driven insane. They quit normal life, attracting the ire of polite society.

FIRST LINE IN PERSIAN: *kār-i ʿāshiq tarāna guftan bāshad*

MY LIPS ARE DRY, BUT IF THEY'RE WET BY YOU,
our love will make me tear apart the lands.
If you would give me but a single kiss,
I'd bow before your feet and clap my hands.

SAVORING
LOVE

LAST NIGHT MY LOVE WAS LIKE THE MOON
   ABOVE.
No, he's a beauty brighter than the sun.
He lies beyond the compass of my mind.
I cannot liken him to anyone.

NOTE: Rumi believes that the tongue and human speech inevitably
fall short of describing the beloved.

FIRST LINE IN PERSIAN: *dosh ān but-i man hamchū mah-i gardūn būd*

IN HOPES IT WOULD FORGET PAST LOVE,
my heart drinks new wine day by day.
He brews the wine of love and then
pours it to take my sense away.

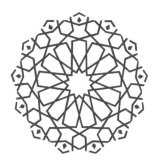

FIRST LINE IN PERSIAN: *har roz dilam naw shikarī nosh kunad*

WHEN YOU ARE HERE, I CLAP WITH JOY.
And when you're gone, I bite my hand.
All I can do is think of you,
so I will do what you command.

FIRST LINE IN PERSIAN: *bar bū-yi wafā dast zanānat bāsham*

YOU ARE THE ONE WHO GIVES THE HEAVENS JOY.

If humans love you too, does that surprise?

As long as I should live, I am your slave.

Call me—I'll come or not, as you advise.

TWO LOVERS TALK WITHOUT A TONGUE.

My words are hidden from all ears.

No one will hear my speech but you,

though I may speak among our peers.

NOTE: Lover and beloved communicate through means that rise above our mundane, audible speech. Their hearts are as one. Everything is felt mutually. Before the feeling is formulated into words, it is already understood. See the note on page 24.

FIRST LINE IN PERSIAN: *bā tu sukhanān-i be-zabān khwāham guft*

WITHOUT YOU, LIFE'S ḤARĀM* FOR ME, MY
   DEAR.

What life without you can there be, my dear?

I swear by God that life without you is

no more than death (called life), you see, my dear.

* NOTE: Ḥarām means impermissible, illicit, a sin.

FIRST LINE IN PERSIAN: *ay be-tu ḥarām zindagānī ay jān*

YOU'RE LIKE THE MOON. YOU VANISH EVERY
   DAWN
and make me spin in circles, like the sky.
You are a lion and my heart's your prey.
Will liver be the next thing that you try?

NOTE: Like the heart, the liver is a seat of emotion in
West Asian cultures.

FIRST LINE IN PERSIAN: *paywasta mahā ʿazm-i safar me-dārī*

THAT THIEF WHO STOLE MY HEART SHOWED
   ME A PLACE.
The realms of soul and body we surpassed.
I said, "I shall not go!" with some excuse.
He said, "You'll go!" and pulled me there at last.

NOTE: Shams took Rumi to new spiritual heights. The lower
self (*nafs*) will naturally resist this progression into a more
difficult, unknown stage of the Sufi path.

FIRST LINE IN PERSIAN: *khwash jāy ki yār-i dil-sitānam me-barad*

THE BEAUTIES OF THE WORLD ENVY YOUR FACE,
your brows a miḥrāb* where ascetics pray.
I was stripped nude of all my qualities,
so in your river I could swim away.

* NOTE: The *miḥrāb* is a niche in the wall of a mosque that indicates
the direction of prayer, Mecca.

FIRST LINE IN PERSIAN: *ay ḥasrat-i khūbān-i jahān rū-yi khwashat*

WE'RE BROKEN, DRUNK TODAY LIKE EVERY DAY.

Don't worry, rather take a lute and play.

There are a hundred ways to pray and bow

for one who faces beauty as they pray.

NOTE: The beloved's beauty serves the role of a mosque prayer niche, showing the orientation of devotion.

FIRST LINE IN PERSIAN: *imroz chū har roz kharābīm kharāb*

I TAKE A WALK, IT'S TO YOUR LANE.
I play the flute, it's for your sake.
You've been so kind and gracious too.
In death and life, I'm yours to take.

NOTE: Rumi opens the *Masnawī* with a harrowing eighteen couplets about a flute that plays the song of separation.

FIRST LINE IN PERSIAN: *bahr-i tu zanam nawā chū nay bar-gīram*

I NEEDED MY UPLIFTING IDOL, BUT

he teased so much, a beggar I became.

The night drew to an end, but not our talk.

Our talk was long, so is the night to blame?

NOTE: Shams acts so aloof that Rumi begs for his presence. When they finally meet, there is so much to be said. They speak all night and still aren't done conversing.

FIRST LINE IN PERSIAN: *man būdam dosh o ān but-i jān afroz*

I'M BOUND TO YOU WITH LOVE AND LOYALTY,
though all you do is hurt me constantly.
I'm patient, but you feel no shame at all
for all the suffering that you've caused me!

FIRST LINE IN PERSIAN: *chandīn ba tu bar mihr o wafā basta-yi man*

YOUR LOVE'S A PUNISHMENT, SEVERE,*
and lovers are your dagger's prey.
Night falls, and everyone's asleep.
A wolf has snatched my sleep away.

* NOTE: The last three words of the first line are in Arabic, quoted from Qur'an 14:7. The vast majority of Rumi's poetry is in Persian, with the occasional Arabic, Turkish, or even Greek line.

FIRST LINE IN PERSIAN: *ay ʿishq-i tuʾam ʾinna ʿaẕābī lashadīd*

YOU ARE MY EYES. HOW ELSE COULD I SEE
  LIGHT?
You're on my mind. My passion you ignite.
That place you took me—I do not know where—
without love, how could I reach such a height?

FIRST LINE IN PERSIAN: *dar chashm-i manī wagarna bīnā kayamī*

I SAUNTERED IN THE GARDEN WITH MY LOVE.

I chanced to glance upon a rose while there.

"For shame! How dare you!" my belovèd said.

"Why look at roses when my face is here?"

THE DAY I SEE YOU, IT HAS FRIDAY JOY.
Your fortune makes this day unlike the rest.
And if the heavens are my enemies,
it matters not. Your love is in my breast.

NOTE: Friday is the Muslim holy day.

FIRST LINE IN PERSIAN: *rozī ki tu rā bīnam ādīna-yi māst*

OH YOU WHO HAVE BECOME THIS SERVANT'S
   SOUL,
in darkness you became my guiding light.
You start to sing your songs inside my heart,
and dance within my head like wine all night.

MY SOUL AND YOURS HAVE ALWAYS BEEN AS
   ONE,
both what's concealed and that which meets the eye.
It is naive to speak of "mine and yours,"
for there's no mine and yours with you and I.

FIRST LINE IN PERSIAN: *dar aṣl yakī budast jān-i man o tu*

ONE WHO SEES ROSY CHEEKS AND TULIP EYES
will fill the skies and heavens with his cries.
A thousand-year fermented wine won't cause
the madness that a year-old love implies.

FIRST LINE IN PERSIAN: *chasmī ki naẓar badān gul o lāla kunad*

MAY LOVERS BE DRUNK AND DISGRACED ALL
  YEAR.
May they be mad, impassioned, and crazy.
When sober, we fret over everything.
When drunk, we say, "As it is, may it be."

NOTE: Worldly status and reputation are a source of ego and
a barrier for the Sufi.

FIRST LINE IN PERSIAN: *ʿāshiq hama sāl mast o ruswā bādā*

SHALL I GROW TIRED OF YOUR FACE?

    No, no, no!

Or take a new love in your place?

    No, no, no!

Your garden's full of roses, that I see.

Should every thorn stop my embrace?

    No, no, no!

FIRST LINE IN PERSIAN: *jāna zi tu bīzār shawam nay nay nay*

I'VE SEEN NO TREE UPRIGHT LIKE YOU.
I've seen no moon with light like you.
I've seen no sun shine bright like you.
I've seen no sweet delight like you.

FIRST LINE IN PERSIAN: *sar-sabz-tar az tu man nadīdam shajarī*

WHATEVER CRUELTY COMES FROM YOU, MY
   DEAR,
is better than a beauty's loyalty.
Much better in the end than faith, I've found:
the heresies* your love has taught to me.

* NOTE: Laypeople misunderstood Sufi teachings as heretical.

FIRST LINE IN PERSIAN: *har jawr o jafā'ī ki zi tu jān āyad*

NIGHT FALLS, AND FROM THE NIGHT I FEEL
  SUCH JOY.
Tonight there is a guest who shines so bright.
The day and night are not alike in love.
I am not bound by either day or night.

NOTE: Sufis move beyond our normal understanding of day, night, hours, and whatever other constructions measure the passage of time. They exist in another realm.

FIRST LINE IN PERSIAN: *be-gāh shud o zi be-gahī man shādam*

WHAT CAN A LOVER DO BUT HUMBLY WAIT?
What can he do at night but come to you?
If he should kiss your curls, don't be upset.
If madmen don't bite chains, what should they do?

NOTE: See the note on page 29.

FIRST LINE IN PERSIAN: *'āshiq ki tawāżu' nanimāyad chi kunad*

WITH YOU THE WORLD IS WARM AND FULL OF
  JOY.
You're joy itself. I'm but a part of it.
It's just the sun who gives that to the world,
what many stars and moons cannot emit.

NOTE: *Shams* means *sun* in Persian, via Arabic.

FIRST LINE IN PERSIAN: *ay bā tu jahān ẓarīf o shādī-bāra*

YOU'RE MY TRANQUILITY AND RESTING PLACE.
Misfortunes end when I gaze at your face.
If in your gathering I break a glass,
I'll buy gold goblets—hundreds—in its place.

FIRST LINE IN PERSIAN: *ay rāḥat o āramgah-i paywastam*

ABOUT THE THINGS WE DID LAST NIGHT . . .
they can't be penned or said out loud.
The day I leave this old abode,
you'll hear this story from my shroud.

NOTE: Muslims are buried in a simple white shroud.

FIRST LINE IN PERSIAN: *dosh ānchi biraft dar miyān-i man o tu*

MAY MY HEART NEVER BE QUIT OF YOUR FACE,
or be quit of your never-ending grace.
If you see a bramble growing from my grave,
those thorns will also itch for your embrace.

NOTE: In Persian, the verb *to itch* (*khārīdan*) comes from the word *thorn* (*khār*).

FIRST LINE IN PERSIAN: *ḥāshā ki dilam tark-i ʿiẕār-i tu kunad*

MY SOUL HAS BEEN ECSTATIC FOR SOME TIME.

They point at me and laugh: "He's gone insane!"

To die and leave this world is not a thing.

The problem is to rise and leave your lane.

FIRST LINE IN PERSIAN: *'umrīst ki jān-i banda be-khweshtan ast*

ALL SOULS WHO DRINK THE POTION OF YOUR
  LOVE
will rise. Oh water of life, how they will rise!
Death smelled me, but he only found your scent.
Death let me go and now averts his eyes.

FIRST LINE IN PERSIAN: *az sharbat-i sawdā-yi tu har jān ki mazīd*

THAT HEART I THOUGHT BELONGED TO ME . . .
(Trust it to someone? How could I?)
Oh love, it left me. Now it's yours.
Take care of it, as once would I!

FIRST LINE IN PERSIAN: *ān dil ki man ān-i khwesh pindāshtam*

THE ONE WITH AN ALLURING, ENVIED FACE
came late at night to weep upon my heart.
We wept together 'til the morning broke.
Who could tell lover or beloved apart?

NOTE: See the note on page 13.

FIRST LINE IN PERSIAN: *ān kas ki ba rū-yi khūb ū rashk-i parīst*

MY DEAR, THE NIGHT HAS PASSED, YET HERE I
   AM.
My yearning pleas and grief are here to stay.
You are my light at dawn and sleep at night.
Without you, may there be no night or day.

FIRST LINE IN PERSIAN: *shab raft o naraft ay but-i sīmīn-bar-i man*

FROM LOVING YOU, THERE'S LIGHT IN EVERY
   HEART
and humble prayers read in every pew.
We need a lengthy night and shining moon,
just to explain the pain that's caused by you.

NOTE: Lovers meet at night. In this case, it must be a long night
(such as one in winter) with a bright, full moon, so that Rumi has
enough time to explain all the pain Shams has caused him.

FIRST LINE IN PERSIAN: *ay dar dil-i har kasī zi mihrat tābī*

I SAID, "I WILL UPROOT MY HEART FROM YOU."

But oh! I can't.

I said, "I will forget my grief awhile."

But no, I can't.

I said, "I'll drive this yearning from my heart."

But how can I?

If I was man enough for that, I would.

Alas, I can't.

FIRST LINE IN PERSIAN: *guftam ki dil az tu bar-kanam natwānam*

MY LOVE WAS BOTHERED BY A VERSE I READ.

"With meter you can't measure me," he said.

I answered, "Why lay waste to what I wrote?"

"A verse cannot contain me. You're misled."

NOTE: Shams defies description. Rumi dismissed requests to speak about Shams in detail, relate his teachings, or disclose what transpired between them.

FIRST LINE IN PERSIAN: *bar guftam bayt dil-bar az man ranjīd*

SINCE I BECAME CONSUMED BY LOVE FOR YOU,
my poor heart fell to sorrow and dismay.
So many times I felt the pain of love,
but not the misery I feel today.

FIRST LINE IN PERSIAN: *tā bā gham-i ʿishq-i tu marā kār uftād*

YOU KILL YOUR LOVERS FOR A SMALL OFFENSE.

Not only lovers! Confidants you slay.

Forget we're friends. Consider me a foe.

Would any person kill their foes this way?

FIRST LINE IN PERSIAN: *ay dost ba har sukhan kasī yār kushad*

OH IDOL, YOU COME NICELY, FRESH OF FACE.

Were you not happy with the heart you stole?

You smile and sting me with your ruby lips.

Why have you now come back to take my soul?

FIRST LINE IN PERSIAN: *khwash khwash ṣanamā tāza-rukhān āmada'ī*

I DO NOT HAVE THE HANDS TO SHED YOUR
   BLOOD,
nor feet to walk with patience on your way.
You cannot tolerate this slave of yours,
and I don't have the sense to run away.

FIRST LINE IN PERSIAN: *nay dast ki dar maṣāf khūn-rez kunīm*

MOURNING
LOVE

JUST YESTERDAY, THE SOUL HAD JOY AND LIGHT.
Today, the flame of love burns it away.
Alas, 'twas written in our book of fate:
joy yesterday and pain for us today.

FIRST LINE IN PERSIAN: *day būd chūnān dawlat o jān afrozī*

OH LORD, GIVE HIM A CRUEL BELOVED
that thirsts for blood and steals hearts too.
Give love to him, give love to him,
so he will feel the pain we knew.

NOTE: The beloved is often called a *heart-ravisher* (*dil-rubā*) and *heart-taker* (*dil-bar*).

FIRST LINE IN PERSIAN: *yā rabb tu yakī yār-i jafā-kārash dih*

I HID THE WINE, BUT I CAN'T HIDE THE SMELL.
Nor can I hide my wine-sick look, it seems.
I dry my lips to make my love look dry,
but what to do with eyes that flow like streams?

FIRST LINE IN PERSIAN: *gar bāda nahān kunīm bū rā chi kunīm*

WITH EVERY BREATH HE PAINS MY AILING
  HEART.
His heart is stone! Oh, why won't he take heed?
I wrote my story with these bloody tears.
He saw it, but he did not care to read.

SINCE GOD HAS WRITTEN, WE MUST PART.

Why do we fight, fear His decree?

Remember me if I am good.

And if I'm not, you're free from me.

NOTE: Rumi believes we must resign ourselves to divine will and
see the good in everything. If you part from a lover, you can think
of it two ways. If the relationship was unhealthy, you are relieved.
If it was a good relationship, you can remember it fondly. As Alfred,
Lord Tennyson famously wrote, "'Tis better to have loved and lost
than never to have loved at all."

FIRST LINE IN PERSIAN: *chūn zūd nibishta būd ḥaqq furqat-i mā*

WHEN I FIRST HEARD THE TALE OF LOVERS
   TOLD,
in love's pursuit I lost my soul and heart.
I thought, perhaps my love and I were two,
no! We were one, though I thought us apart.

NOTE: Rumi believes in one love. Lover and beloved are not two or
apart. They are one and together.

FIRST LINE IN PERSIAN: *zawwal ki ḥadīs̱-i ʿāshiqī bishnūdam*

ALAS, YOU DID NOT LIGHT MY HEART.

All that you did was burn and break.

I gave to you my heart and soul.

You took them. They weren't yours to take.*

* NOTE: Literally, "They were not fated or provisioned for you."
Muslims believe everything one is entitled to is predetermined.

FIRST LINE IN PERSIAN: *afsos ki ṭab ʾ-i dil-furozīt nabuwad*

I WON'T BE HOPELESS IF YOU FOUND NEW LOVE,
or if you found another one more fair.
As long as I'm alive, I'll long for you.
There are so many hopes found in despair.

FIRST LINE IN PERSIAN: *nawmed niyam garcha zi man bubrīdī*

MY LOVER IS SO LOYAL THAT
I shed tear after bloody tear!
I say he loves me, like a fool.
He's found new love; that much is clear.

FIRST LINE IN PERSIAN: *dar 'ahd o wafā chunān ki dil-dār-i manast*

YOU LEFT, OH IDOL, BUT TWO THINGS REMAIN:
our love and my mind's constant thoughts of you.
I wander 'round, hoping we will cross paths.
Life's way is twisted; you guided me through.

FIRST LINE IN PERSIAN: *raftī o naraft ay but-i bugzīda-yi man*

WHEN I WAS WITH YOU, LOVE KEPT ME AWAKE.
Without you, all I did was cry 'til day.
Praise be to God, both nights I could not sleep.
These sleepless nights were not the same, were they?

FIRST LINE IN PERSIAN: *tā bā tu buwam nakhuspam az yārī-hā*

YOU SAID, "COME, WHILE THE SPRING AND
  GARDEN BLOOM.
Here there are wine and beauties, come and see!"
But those are of no use if you're not there.
And if you're there, what good are those to me?

TONIGHT I'M JOINED BY SOMEONE NEW, NOT
  YOU.
A garden banquet, set so beautifully:
wine, sweets, and candles. Melodies as well.
If only they were gone and you with me.

FIRST LINE IN PERSIAN: *imshab manam o yakī ḥarīfī chū manī*

THOSE SWEET THINGS YOU AND I WOULD SAY
are hidden in the heavens' heart.
Our secrets will rain down one day
and grow all 'round this worldly court.

FIRST LINE IN PERSIAN: *ān khwash sukhanān ki mā biguftīm ba ham*

YOU LEFT, AND I'VE SHED TEARS OF BLOOD
  SINCE THEN,
and your increasing sorrows draw my cries.
No! When you left, my eyes went after you.
How can I weep if I possess no eyes?

FIRST LINE IN PERSIAN: *raftī waz raftan-i tu man khūn giryam*

A LOVER THAT MERE WORDS CANNOT DESCRIBE
would ask about my poor heart as it bled.
His long robe touched the ground. My heart declared:
"Pull up your robe! The ground is bloodied red!"

FIRST LINE IN PERSIAN: *yārī ki ba ḥusn az ṣifat afzūnast*

OH DEAR DAWN BREEZE,* PLEASE BLOW MY
  LOVER'S WAY.
If he's content, speak of my poor heart's state.
But if his mood is bad, then be aware.
You saw me not. There's nothing to relate.

* NOTE: In Persian poetry, the early morning zephyr is a messenger
for lovers.

FIRST LINE IN PERSIAN: *ay bād-i saḥar ba sū-yi ān dil-bar kash*

MY HEART REMEMBERS YOU. I LOSE MY SENSE!

Without your sweet lips, how can I sip wine?

To see your face, my eyes can only hope.

To hear your voice, my ears can only pine.

THE MAN WHO HAS NO MATCH IN BEAUTY LEFT
(though by his sight I wasn't satisfied).
He left, but grief for him remained in me.
The thorn remains, although the rose has dried.

FIRST LINE IN PERSIAN: *raft ānki nabwad kas ba khūbī yārash*

MY HEART FOR WANT OF YOU IS AS A LUTE.

Your fire has burned its every part away.

My lover doesn't speak about my pain.

What silence says, his words cannot convey.

FIRST LINE IN PERSIAN: *dil az hawas-i tu chūn rubāb ast rubāb*

OH DAY BY DAY, MY HEART ACHES WITH YOUR
  PAIN.
Your ruthless heart is wearied more of me.
You left me, but your sorrow does remain.
Your sorrow shows to me more loyalty.

FIRST LINE IN PERSIAN: *har roz dilam dar gham-i tu zār-tar ast*

MY HEART THUMPS WHEN I THINK OF YOU,

while bloody tears drip down my breast.

Whenever there is news of you,

my poor heart flies out of my chest!

AT TIMES, OUR SEPARATION BURNED MY WORLD.

And other times, joy set my soul aflame.

Alas that destiny wrote fate like this:

One day is joy, the next is not the same.

FIRST LINE IN PERSIAN: *gāhī buwadam furqat-i ʿālam-sozī*

THEY ASK ME, "WHY ARE YOU IN SUCH DEEP
  PAIN?
What is this sallow face? Why shout and cry?"
I say, "Don't ask me why I am this way.
Look at his moon face,* and you will know why!"

* NOTE: The lover's face is likened to the moon, which is round
and full of light.

FIRST LINE IN PERSIAN: *goyand marā ki īn hama dard chirāst*

YOU THINK I'M OVER YOU? I'M NOT!
I won't be calm until my death.
(Oh Lord, do not let me feel joy
if I forget him for one breath!)

FIRST LINE IN PERSIAN: *me-pindārī ki az ghamānat rastam*

LAST NIGHT I THOUGHT, "HIS ABSENCE IS
  UNJUST!"
(While agitated by our time apart.)
Your memory is here, though you are not.
While sleeping, thoughts of you will calm my heart.

FIRST LINE IN PERSIAN: *man dosh firāq rā jafā me-guftam*

I DID NOT THINK YOU WOULD EXPEL ME FROM
your heart—my bags left in the mud—and go.
To foe and friend I boasted of you once.
Don't leave me shamed before both friend and foe.

FIRST LINE IN PERSIAN: *dar dil naguẕasht kaz dilam bugẕārī*

MY LOVE CAME BACK, BUT WITH A HEART OF
  STONE.
And with his stone, he tore my heart apart.
I was with him; his love made me a harp.*
He struck me with his claws. Alas, my heart!

NOTE: Rumi likens the beloved to the humbly bent-over harp,
which cries out when plucked by the cruel beloved. In Persian,
chang means both *harp* and *claw*.

FIRST LINE IN PERSIAN: *bāz āmad yār bā dilī chūn khāra*

THE DAY WHEN MY SOUL WANTS TO LEAVE
  THIS WORLD
and my whole body starts to break apart,
write with your finger on the dirt: *Get up!*
I'll leave the grave with a new soul and heart.

FIRST LINE IN PERSIAN: *ān roz ki jānam rah-i kaywān gīrad*

I DIED LAMENTING LOVE. BREATHE ME TO LIFE,

for by your breath I'll live forevermore.

You said we would be sharing every breath.

You lied. Don't you feel guilty anymore?

BEAR OFF MY BODY WHEN I DIE.
Entrust me to my lover then.
If he should kiss my withered lips,
I will come back to life again.

FIRST LINE IN PERSIAN: *gar man bimuram marā biyārīd shumā*

I WENT TO MY BELOVÈD'S BLESSÈD GRAVE.

He shone beneath the mud, a flower bed.

I pleaded with the earth and warned, "Beware!

Take good care of the loyal, loving dead!"

FIRST LINE IN PERSIAN: *raftam ba sar-i gūr-i karīm-i dil-dār*

INDEX OF FIRST LINES
IN ENGLISH

INDEX OF FIRST LINES
IN PERSIAN

AUTHOR'S NOTE

If you enjoyed this volume, follow @persianpoetics on Instagram and X (formerly Twitter) for more translations. Courses on this book and Rumi's other works are available at www.persianpoetics.com.

ABOUT THE AUTHOR

Muhammad Ali Mojaradi is a scholar, teacher, and translator of Persian poetry. In 2020, he launched @persianpoetics and created the #rumiwasmuslim campaign, attracting international media attention. Mojaradi has been interviewed in HuffPost and the Middle East Monitor, and on Al Jazeera's *The Listening Post*, among many others. This is his first book.

MANDALA

An Imprint of MandalaEarth
PO Box 3088
San Rafael, CA 94912
www.MandalaEarth.com

Find us on Facebook: www.facebook.com/MandalaEarth

Publisher Raoul Goff
Associate Publisher Roger Shaw
Publishing Director Katie Killebrew
Editor Peter Adrian Behravesh
Assistant Editor Amanda Nelson
VP, Creative Director Chrissy Kwasnik
Art Director Ashley Quackenbush
Production Designer Amy Tang
VP Manufacturing Alix Nicholaeff
Senior Production Manager Joshua Smith
Senior Production Manager, Subsidiary Rights Lina s Palma-Temena

MandalaEarth would also like to thank Bob Cooper.

Text © 2024 Muhammad Ali Mojaradi

ISBN: 979-8-88762-106-7

Manufactured in China by Insight Editions
10 9 8 7 6 5 4 3 2 1

REPLANTED PAPER

Insight Editions, in association with Roots of Peace, will plant two trees for each tree used in the manufacturing of this book. Roots of Peace is an internationally renowned humanitarian organization dedicated to eradicating land mines worldwide and converting war-torn lands into productive farms and wildlife habitats. Roots of Peace will plant two million fruit and nut trees in Afghanistan and provide farmers there with the skills and support necessary for sustainable land use.